12

CATASTROPHE
THE END OF THE CINEMA?

For the audiences of the Atom Age, the fear of the primeval monster is transmuted in *Night of the Blood Beast* (1958) to a creature from outer space who plants his breeding spores in the human bloodstream, while *The Terror Strikes* (1958) is a Bert Gordon special effects film, in which atomic mutation produces a rampaging sixty-foot army officer.

CATASTROPHE
THE END OF THE CINEMA?
David Annan

Bounty Books

CONTENTS

PAGE 7
BORN TO DISASTER

PAGE 34
FIRE, QUAKE, WIND, DROUGHT,
COLD, PLAGUE AND WAR

PAGE 62
IF THE END IS NOT NOW IT IS SOON

PAGE 84
THE END AND THE CINEMA

ACKNOWLEDGEMENTS

The publishers wish to thank the following organizations and people for their help in preparing this book: the British Film Institute, 20th Century Fox, MGM-EMI, Columbia-Warner, United Artists, Allied Artists, Paramount, Universal MCA, RCA General Inc., Rank, First National Cinema International Corporation, Hammer, the Cinema Bookshop, Anglo-Amalgamated, AIP, Contemporary Films, British Lion, Hemdale, Intercontinental Films, the stills and information departments of the National Film Archives, Titan International, Don Getz, Al Reuter, Brian McIlmail and Martin Jones and Hieronymus Bosch

BORN TO DISASTER

Gwangi **represents the primeval fears of men at all times.**

The human race has always lived on the edge of catastrophe. When we existed in the woods and caves, every day was a battle for survival. Famine could wipe out the little tribes of primeval men and women. So could plague, or cold, or forest fire, or volcano, or earthquake, or flood, or any of the natural disasters possible on the cooling globe. If the elements seemed ready to destroy men totally, so did the giant beasts of prehistory, the monsters whose bones now amaze us in the museums and whose visions lurch their menace across the special effects of the screen. Added to the threat of a cruel natural world and of actual beasts, men fought each other to extermination, the cruellest of the species in its search for living at all costs. As the Lorenz and Ardrey books have shown, aggression is a basic drive in us all. If we do not fight for our lives,

Count Zaroff and his henchmen hunt human prey in the swamp in *The Most Dangerous Game* (1931) . . . and the dying Count fires his last arrow.

we will all be annihilated. And even if we no longer need to fight, the fear of total destruction still keeps us aggressive.

Our survival is, after all, the thing most important to us. The biggest catastrophe to any individual is the loss of his own life. The major theme of most adventure films is a series of threats on the life of the hero or heroine, which they manage to surmount, while we feel a cosy thrill at being safe while they are in danger. At its most primitive level, survival movies are concerned with the hunt of men by man and beasts, as in the archetype of them all, *The Most Dangerous Game*, where the lovers are hunted like game through the swamp. Some films are more concerned with survival in the natural wilderness, such as Cornell Wilde's underrated *The Running Man*, and Nicholas Roeg's *Walkabout*. Others are concerned with survival at the crash of human society, such as the early Garbo film, *Joyless Street*, or the Ford version of the plight of the dustbound Okies in Steinbeck's *The Grapes of Wrath*, or Kurosawa's moving work of degradation in his version of Gorki's *The Lower Depths*. Our preoccupation with our own daily existence makes us fear everything from a little domestic disaster, like a scalding kettle, to

Garbo walks out into *The Joyless Street* (1925) to become a prostitute to keep her family together in ruined Vienna.

Henry Fonda tries to keep his family together in John Ford's *The Grapes of Wrath* (1940) as migrants to the shanties of California.

The Queen of Gomorrah arrogantly uses a slave as a footstool before the destruction of the city by fire and brimstone in the Italian *Sodom and Gomorrah* (1962).

the financial collapse of our urban civilisation. We also may fear the literal end of the world through the folly of men and atomic explosion, or even a cosmic disaster of the collision of the planets.

While these terrors of absolute catastrophe have been pushed back into the unconscious of most civilised people, primitive men still are daily scared of the millenium. When the conqueror Alexander the Great met his first Celts to the north of Greece, he asked them what they feared most, expecting the answer to be Alexander the Great. But their chief fear was that the sky might crack and fall on their heads. For this reason they spent time on sacrificing to the gods. So it was with the Hebrews and other ancient peoples. They feared the wrath of God from the sky, the total obliteration of the Cities of the Plain for their sins, or of the submerging of the whole earth in a Flood. In early Christianity, the Second

Coming of Christ was expected any day, when the earth would be destroyed, the graves would be opened, the blessed arise to the Kingdom of Heaven, and sinners be consigned to an everlasting Hell. Such millenial beliefs still survive in the cargo cults of New Guinea, where some of the tribes build wickerwork aeroplanes, hoping to attract a food-bearing God down to earth to solve all their problems of survival.

The Middle Ages of Europe particularly believed in calamity. Times of civil war or plague led to the rise of mobs certain that the end of the World was at hand. In these last days:

'Plague ruled the common people and overthrew images,
The earth quaked. The people of the Jews is burnt,
A strange multitude of half-naked men beat themselves.'

This woodcut of The Last Judgement is taken from the *Liber Cronicarum* of 1493. Grave-opening and the raising of the dead has remained a popular theme in movies.

One film above all captures these troubled times, *The Seventh Seal*, Ingmar Bergman's masterpiece about the self-hatred and cruel puritanism and demented belief in the Book of Revelations and in the Day of Judgement, with which medieval man faced disaster. In the Bergman film, the holocaust of the plague is followed by the coming of the Flagellants, who beat themselves into a frenzy of persecution under the leadership of a savage Savonarola of a priest, obsessed with witchcraft. The figure of Death does actually walk the earth and plays chess with the questing Knight, and the final image of the film is the Dance of Death, with the Grim Reaper leading away on the rim of the world the last of the human race – except

The Flagellants beat themselves about the Cross . . . their leader prays to the tortured Christ . . . then he tortures the suspected witch in the stocks . . . and she ends up on the Cross herself to extirpate the sins that have brought down the wrath of God on the world.

The Dance of Death at the end of *The Seventh Seal* comes from the medieval fear of total annihilation.

for the little family of clowns which the Knight has allowed to escape Death by cheating at chess.

This medieval fear of absolute destruction was summed up in the figures from the Book of Revelations, the *Four Horsemen of the Apocalypse*, often characterised as Death, Famine, Slaughter (or Pestilence) and War. In its first version, starring the wooden Valentino, a bearded Messianic stranger has a vision of the Four Horsemen that seems to have little to do with the cardboard characterisations of the film. Once during a showing of the movie at the National Film Theatre, the sepia film actually became real as the projection booth caught fire, just as Valentino engaged in a death-grapple with his cousin in shell-torn No Man's Land. The audience naturally panicked and rushed for the exit, fearing to be caught in the smoke and blaze of a Cinema Inferno, and life mimicked art at a minimal level. The unconscious fear of catastrophe became real as the Horsemen actually set on fire the silver nitrate illusion. Yet as a film, neither version of the Four Horsemen could put a match to the devastation shown in Milestone's *All Quiet on the Western Front* or Pabst's *Westfront, 1918*.

The Four Horsemen rampage through the skies in howling and woe in this woodcut by Hans Burgkmair from a German New Testament of 1523.

A contemporary French postcard shows the Hun as the Great Destroyer . . .

Pabst's soldier runs out to die in No Man's Land.

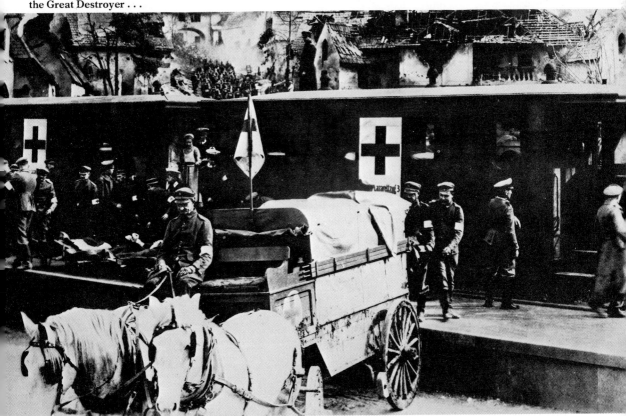

. . . while Milestone's later reconstruction shows the ambulances leaving the devastated town in Northern France.

Other medieval legends allowed the satisfying illusion of mass destruction on the screen. Murnau's extraordinary *Faust* – imitated later by an episode in Disney's *Fantasia* – showed the Devil as large as a mountain with a whole German town caught up in the lower folds of his black and monstrous cloak. Lang's *Krienhild's Revenge* showed the destruction of the Great Hall attacked by the Mongols and defended to the bitter end by the Germans, fulfilling the curse of the Nibelungs. Another success of the early German cinema, also dependent on a medieval legend of destruction, was Wegener's *The Golem*. There the Jewish ghetto, faced by a pogrom from the Emperor, is saved by the cabbalistic Rabbi Löw, who creates a clay monster called the Golem. Like an anti-Sampson, the Golem saves the Emperor and his Court from the ruins of the collapsing palace, and turns in an orgy of fire and destruction on its own creators. Wegener thus created the reverse myth of cinematic catastrophe, that it can be caused by the creators as much as the destroyers.

The Devil looms over the sky in Murnau's *Faust* (1926).

The faithful Hagen defends his master to the last in the burning Hall in *Kriemhild's Revenge* (1924).

The Nibelungs hold up their treasure which is stolen and leads to the total destruction of its owners in Lang's *Siegfried* (1922-24).

The monster Golem terrifies the Emperor's knights before saving their master in the collapsing palace.

The Golem menaces its own master's daughter .

The Golem ravages the ghetto, sending the terrified Jews in a mob through the streets, screaming for the blood of their saviour, turned destroyer.

The ikon of Jacob's Ladder was from St Catherine's Abbey in Sinai, while the woodcut of the torturer of the damned comes from *Le Grant Kalendrier et Compost des Bergiers* of 1496.

These poles of salvation and annihilation were, above all, the dialectic of Christianity as well as a basic myth in the cinema. Jacob's Ladder allowed some to reach heaven, others to fall into hell, where they would suffer forever the tortures of the damned. Although the cinema could use Lucifer's regions as a joke in *Hellzapoppin*, it could also treat them as a place of terror in the many versions made of Dante's Inferno. Yet the power of damnation to terrify men steadily eroded with the growth of a mechanical and materialistic civilisation after the industrial revolution. Hell soon came to be what Sartre was to call it – 'other people'. No Inferno could be worse than that which man made for himself, no Last Judgement greater than that of World War.

It is not a coincidence that the Cinema of Catastrophe coincided with the spread of

Hell is still convenient for the modern cinema, either as a joke in *Hellzapoppin'* (1941) where Frankenstein's monster stops for a chat on his way up from the wetter regions, or as a spectacle in *Dante's Inferno* of 1935 and 1966.

Rien ne résiste au temps.
Nichts kann der Zeit widerstehen.

the methods of human destruction. The fantasies of Jules Verne and H. G. Wells, which inspired the earlier catastrophe films of the French cinema, conceived of man-made as well as natural disasters. For instance, the postcards of the time, which so much influenced the pioneer work of Méliès and the German Expressionists and the French Surrealist Cinema, show 'The Modern Pyramids' of skulls at the close of the Russo-Japanese War of 1905 and Time as the Great Destroyer, sweeping up even the destruction of War. A popular montage series still harped on the Flood with its early special effects, showing L'Opéra in Paris and the Municipal Buildings in Birmingham surrounded by water. Méliès, a stage conjuror, used this montage world of the new moving pictures to show human projectiles giving the moon one in the eye, an apocalyptic

If Birmingham were Venice—Municipal Buildings

coach terrifying its traveller, and even a simulated volcanic eruption. The audiences could enjoy catastrophe as fantasy in the cinema – and destruction as a dream.

Yet destruction was not a dream in the First World War, nor was Death or Famine or even the Pestilence of influenza that killed as many tens of millions of people as the war did. It seemed as if the Christians of Europe had gone mad with destruction and that their God had abandoned them to their man-made Armageddon. Catastrophe was now a reality, even if cinema was the apostle of the unreal.

Méliès' world was full of catastrophe and fantasy, showing his training in magic and theatrical spectacle. The stills come from his *Voyage à la Lune, The Merry Frolics of Satan,* and his *L'Eruption du Mont Pelée.* In the new cult of catastrophe pictures, this last subject is being remade under the title of *The Day the World Ended.*

« Parce que tu as mis toute ta confiance en tes ouvrages, je retirerai ma main de toi; et tu seras réduite. »
(Jeremie Ch 46 27)

A contemporary French postcard quotes Jeremiah's prophecy of God abandoning man because of his faith in his own works.

"YOU'RE NEXT"
SAY THE DICTATORS!
BUT ARE WE?

Paramount Pictures

Paramount's GREAT PICTURE FOR THE DEMOCRACIES!

WORLD IN FLAMES

SCREEN'S MOST EARTH SHAKING DRAMA
...the drama we are living today!

So the possibility of the human race totally destroying itself became one of the first of the cinematic genres, which exploited the innate sense of human catastrophe. After all, it seemed probable by the 1930s that Fascism and modern weapons had achieved the capacity of the Armageddon once reserved for the wrathful hands of God. Paramount's *World in Flames* of 1938 was a newsreel catalogue of the devastation caused by human beings on their own works; the advertisements called it the 'Screen's Most Earth Shaking Drama . . . the drama we are living today!'. Although its message was that democracy could overcome dictatorship, few thought so after the early Axis successes of the Second World War. The blitz documentaries of Grierson and Jennings seemed to show clearly that we could totally destroy our own cities, something prophesied at the opening of H. G. Wells's *Things to Come*, and commemorated from the truth of the Dresden fire-raid in Vonnegut's *Slaughterhouse Five*. Yet the actual dropping of the atom bomb on Hiroshima and Nagasaki proved that the fantasy of an aerial holocaust of 1937 had become the terminal deed of war of 1945.

After the atomic war, the balance of terror between America and Russia preserved the world from catastrophe by human destruction – yet the daily fact of everyone's life had become absolute annihilation. It was no longer the ridiculous fear of a primitive people or the religious frenzy of the Middle Ages; it was and it is the categorical impera-

The blitz sequence from Humphrey Jennings, *Fires Were Started* (1943).

The prophetic destruction of Everytown by the new weapons of war from *Things to Come* (1936).

Billy Pilgrim and other American prisoners-of-war are marched through the doomed city of Dresden in *Slaughterhouse Five* (1972).

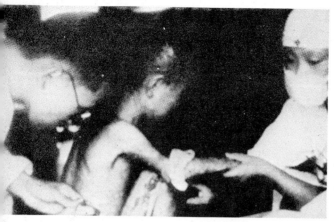

The treatment of the survivors of the atomic blast is intercut with the bed-scene of the lovers in *Hiroshima Mon Amour* (1959), where the dust of that searing past pollutes the love of today.

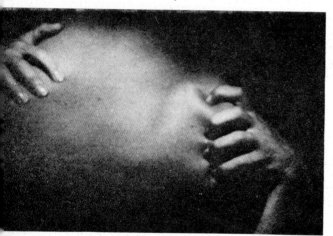

tive behind the uneasy peace of our time. A cinematic genius like Alain Resnais might use Hiroshima both to advance the grammar of film by the use of the time flashback and to protest that love should be more important than the pollution of war or revenge. Another cinematic genius like Stanley Kubrick might present the atomic bomb and the explosion of the world as a black farce, but the fact remains that we can now wipe out our species today, if we wish. Apocalypse is in our own hands. The Four Horsemen now pull our motorcoach to our chosen End of the World. Obliteration is ours, saith Man. Thus the cinema audience need no longer indulge its fantasies of catastrophe – the world which man has made creates catastrophes galore. In fact, even before this era of imminent destruction, history had supplied enough human débâcles to keep the cinema of spectacle employed for ever. The battle sequences in early Italian epics on Napoleon and Hannibal, the carnage in *The Birth of a Nation*, culminated in the recreation of the American civil war in *Gone with the Wind*, where the extras littered the earth as the wounded while Atlanta burned furiously in an orgy of devastation.

The Italian cinema had always pioneered in the techniques of destruction, influencing D. W. Griffith and Eisenstein with its use of mobs and spectacle and flames and crashing pillars. Already by 1908, Maggi's version of *The Last Days of Pompeii* provoked an Italian critic into praising 'the terror of the fleeing spectators, suffocated by the terrible effects of molten lava'. Two more versions of the destruction of Pompeii were filmed in 1913 to capitalise on the world-wide success of the first version of *Quo Vadis?* where Nero's burning of Rome had been received with enthusiasm everywhere. The Italian film tradition has always depended on historical extravaganza and the big final scene; this has always been one of natural or human disaster – from Patrone's *The Fall of Troy*,

Even more horrific images of the destruction of mankind can be seen in Resnais' *Night and Fog*, a documentary on the German concentration camps which killed six million Jews. Here are the terminal mass lavatories.

Dr. Strangelove is subtitled *How I Learned to Love the Bomb*.

The scenes of the burning of Atlanta and of the wounded lying at the railroad station from *Gone With the Wind* (1939) have rarely been equalled in the history of war cinema.

The luxurious lady awaits destruction in Caserini's *The Last Days of Pompeii* (1913).

The mob strips the courtesan in *Cabiria* in the decadent days of Ancient Rome. The tradition of destruction has run all the way through the Italian cinema to such modern spectacles as *The Fall of the Roman Empire* (1964).

The smoking machines threaten to explode – then do, loosing the water in *Metropolis* (1926).

The hero tries to save the children in the underground workers' city.

which forced itself against opposition onto the American market in 1912, through the many versions of Nero's arson of Rome to the struggle against Hannibal in *Cabiria*, where Maciste (that Tarzan of North Italy) always breaks everything in sight in defence of the virtue of the heroine in white.

The German Expressionist cinema also delighted in and exploited the human wish to see the catastrophe of others. Few films have ever equalled the scale and terror of the destruction of the worker's underground city by mechanical explosions and floods in Lang's *Metropolis* of 1926, where the workers abandon their children to an underwater tomb as they follow the *agent provocateur*, the robot Maria. The use of that most Biblical and archetypal terror, drowning under the earth, contributed greatly to the success of the film, which otherwise staggered under the weight of its own message and grandiose overacting. Its sheer scale of devastation was its triumph.

Director Fritz Lang orchestrates the hands reaching up for survival.

The railwaymen watch the train fall into the floods in *Other Men's Women* (1931).

If the fluid sequences in *Metropolis* owed something to the success of the mass drowning of Pharoah's army in the first of the de Mille versions of *The Ten Commandments* (1923), its own success bred imitations in the submerging of the whole world's population in *Noah's Ark* in 1928, in the train disaster toppling into the floods of Wellman's melodramatic *Other Men's Women* of 1931, and in the extraordinary disaster sequence in the British spectacular of 1934, *The Tunnel*, where a transatlantic undersea road is to be built by a vast radium drill. While deep under the ocean, the tunnellers strike a bed of volcanic lava, which explodes. Water and deadly gases menace the whole project, which the originator only drives through at the cost of his son's life.

The transatlantic tunnel of the future menaces all with watery destruction.

In *The Dam Busters* the tension slowly builds in the bomber until the final raid, when the dam busts.

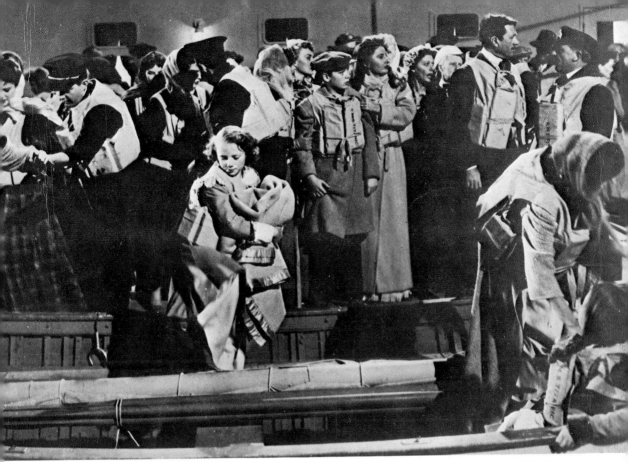

There is very little tension in the first version of *Titanic* with Clifton Webb and Robert Wagner and Barbara Stanwyck.

Yet perhaps the most spectacular flood scenes are not the underwater tomb sequences – so exploited in the successful submarine and sinking liner epics of today – but the recreations of the burning of dams or the coming of tidal waves, when mobs and cities are swept up in walls of killing water. Louis Bromfield's successful novel, *When the Rains Came*, was made into a film. It builds up sexual and racial tension in Ranchipur in India, until torrential rains and an earthquake cause the breaking of the great dam and the ruin of the city with casts of thousands caught in the deluge. The plague in the shape of cholera then strikes the devastated city and kills its ruling Maharani, but allows redemption to the drunkard in his work among the sick. Catastrophe is not always bad for everyone.

The other great spectacle of the crashing down of the waters was done deliberately by the Royal Air Force, recreating the episode of the successful raid on the Ruhr dams in *The Dam Busters* of 1955. The excitement of the catastrophe for the viewers lay in the slow and deliberate planning for the denouement, the setting up of a special air squadron, the invention of a new bomb that could bounce along the surface of the water, the psychological tension leading up to the final attack. In the genre of catastrophe pictures, the slow building of suspense is a vital element, and the plotting of future destruction is almost as exciting as the sight of the disaster itself. In fact, most of a catastrophe film deals with the prolonged count-down to the débâcle. Large-scale disaster is usually too expensive to keep up its ruin for ninety minutes.

The first great catastrophe in the Bible was the Flood, and death by water still remains a primal terror. We are born in a watery sack and our escape from it is into our life. To return to it, trapped in an underground chamber, provokes hysteria and claustrophobia. This was brilliantly exploited in the best of Kenneth More's films, *A Night to Remember* (1958), about the

TITANIC...
the greatest sea disaster in living memory

sinking of the *Titanic*, where the shots of the lighted ballroom, submerging under the rising ocean, seem like a true requiem for a civilisation going down. The recent world-wide successes of *The Poseidon Adventure* followed by *Juggernaut* show that movies about human beings, trapped in narrow passageways by water and threatened with drowning, strike a phobia deep in the mass consciousness. Birth is the first release into life from water, the matter of life. Death by water remains the worst threat of all, the suffocation of all that we have known.

The *Titanic* sinks from an iceberg – and no help comes.

Fire and flood menace the passengers in *The Poseidon Adventure*.

Crew and passengers are trapped in the *Poseidon Adventure* (opposite and above)

Explosions rock the liner in *Juggernaut*.

Of all deaths by drowning, perhaps Clouzot showed the most unbearable in his brilliant *Wages of Fear*, when his hero nearly drowns in oil.

FIRE, QUAKE, WIND, DROUGHT, COLD, PLAGUE AND WAR

Robert Frost once started a poem with the words that some said the world would end in fire and some in ice. Fire is a more popular cataclysm in the cinema, because of its fierceness and leaping and danger, while the world of ice must be rather frozen. Méliès did produce a monstrous apparition in his early version of a voyage to the North Pole; but on the whole, volcanoes provided more catastrophe than glaciers, and Etna proved more of a menace than Everest.

A monster rises out of the ice to meet the explorers in Méliès' film, *The Conquest of the Pole* (1912).

The boredom of climbing mountains in Japan had to be made interesting by the appearance of a huge Abominable Snowman in *Half Human* (1955).

The famous chariot-race in the original American *Ben Hur* (1926).

The Last Days of Pompeii remained the favourite spectacle in the cinema in Italy. By 1926, it had been made five times, although Carmine Gallone's version of that year was certainly the biggest and the best to date, with a cast of 5,000 extras for the circus sequence and a cost of 7,000,000 lire. In fact, after the failure of the mammoth *Quo Vadis?* of the year before, Gallone's volcano to end all volcanoes proved the final explosion beneath the tottering finances of the early Italian film industry. As a contemporary critic wrote: 'This was the last important film to be shot in Italy. Instead of the *The Last Days of Pompeii* it could almost have been called The Last Days of the Italian Cinema'. Despite tinting in blue for the night sequences and red for the rain of fire from the volcano, the film was a box-office débâcle and left the Italian cinema penniless and in the hands of Mussolini as his 'most powerful weapon'.

That same year, the American *Ben Hur* won the spectacle stakes with its huge naval battle and chariot-race sequence. In Wyler's remake of 1959, the sensation of drowning in the flaming slave-galleys is as frightening as any flood picture, the fire and the water offering a double death of horror. Yet in spectacle, nothing has equalled the volcanic and tidal wave sequences from Cinerama's

Charlton Heston at the oars of the Roman galley in *Ben Hur* (1959).

In the naval battle in the second *Ben Hur*, there is death by Greek fire or drowning.

Tidal waves and flame destroy the ship in *Krakatoa, East of Java* (1967).

Krakatoa: East of Java, which claimed to be the depiction of 'the most powerful explosion, natural or man-made, in history . . . one-million times more powerful than the largest nuclear device ever detonated'. It recreated the actual explosion of the volcano Krakatoa in the Sunda Strait in 1883, which fired a column of ash and smoke fifty miles into the air and sent a tidal wave seven times round the globe, destroying over 300 towns and villages and 40,000 people. Although the plot-line of the film was weak, its devastating special effects in

Sequence from a Roman camp in the expensive Italian *The Apocalypse* of 1946.

Cinerama were loud and annihilating enough to make it a success with the audiences. *(See Colour Section.)*

Volcanoes, though, are also symbolic of pent-up human emotions. They are a catharsis as much as an apocalypse. In *Volcano* of 1953, the bare island of the title, with its menace of eruption, is symbolic of the seething passions of Anna Magnani, exiled back to her birthplace for being a mainland prostitute and set to work in the pumice mines of cold lava. In the end, ostracised and despised by the village women, she kills her sister's would-be lover to save the young girl from him, then dies in the necessary final explosion of the volcano. The film was too obvious to be successful, but as catastrophe pictures go, it made its point about the parallel between human and natural disaster.

Since the Second World War, the Italian cinema has always run on a divergent course, skidding between the traditional cinema of spectacle and the brilliant neo-realism developed by Rossellini after Italy's defeat. In the same year as *Paisà* and *Shoeshine* (1946), a director called Scotese could conjure enough money out of war-ravaged Rome to make *The Apocalypse*, a parade of nineteen centuries of human history which used even more sets and extras than the greatest spectacle under Mussolini, *The Iron Crown*. Yet the gigantic catastrophe movie had already passed from the hands of the Italians back to Hollywood, its natural domain, and occasionally to England, where the studios and the finance were large enough to cope with the necessary pictorial devastation.

Hollywood was actually built on a potential catastrophe – the San Andreas fault, a crack in the earth subject to earthquake which runs from Los Angeles to North California. A major tremor in the fault caused the destruction of San Francisco in 1906, first by an earthquake and then by a fire that raged among the ruins. Although few more than five hundred people were actually killed in the disaster, the effect was one of total devastation, followed by looting and riots. *(See Colour Section)* With that local

Dix-Huitième année. — N° 900.   Huit pages : CINQ centimes   Dimanche 6 Mai 1906.

Le Petit Parisien

SUPPLÉMENT LITTÉRAIRE ILLUSTRÉ

TOUS LES JOURS
Le Petit Parisien
(Six pages)
5 centimes

CHAQUE SEMAINE
LE SUPPLÉMENT LITTÉRAIRE
5 centimes

DIRECTION: 18, rue d'Enghien (10e). PARIS

ABONNEMENTS
PARIS ET DÉPARTEMENTS:
12 mois, 4 fr. 50. 6 mois, 2 fr. 25
UNION POSTALE:
12 mois, 5 fr. 50. 6 mois, 3 fr

The Militia shoot looters in the devastated streets of San Francisco after the earthquake.

Gable and Tracy in the refugee camp after the earthquake in *San Francisco* (1936).

Ruby Keeler dances amid collapsing New York in *42nd Street*

The Old Master Méliès had already done his earthquake back in 1906 in *Robert Macaire and Bertrand*.

Los Angeles begins to collapse in Mark Robson's *Earthquake* (1974).

The Blazing Tower (1975), with devastating artwork and special effects, is the most recent movie on the subject of skyscraper disasters.

example at the beginning of the American film industry, it is surprising that no major earthquake picture was made in California until *San Francisco* in 1936. In this movie, Clark Gable played the owner of a club on the Barbary Coast, where Jeannette Macdonald sang. He even had to knock down Spencer Tracy, playing the priest who befriended them both, but refused to allow Gable to put Miss Macdonald in a cabaret scene wearing next to nothing. Just as Miss Macdonald left Gable to marry another man, the earthquake happened to put a stop to this impetuous action. The lovers survived, though Gable was felled by a falling brick wall which he shrugged off to the delight of the audience. He was finally only brought down by having to fall to his

knees while Miss Macdonald led a group in singing 'Nearer My God To Thee', which was almost as much of a take-off of the disaster movie as Ruby Keeler singing the title song of Busby Berkeley's *42nd Street* amid the dancing, collapsing skyscrapers of New York. The scale of the production called for some frightening scenes of devastation. The sound of the first rumble, the collapse of complete streets and buildings, the city-wide fire out of control, and the dynamiting of whole blocks to stop it remains a terrifying spectacle. Memories of it and a determination not to repeat the stupidities of the old plot was an inspiration behind Hollywood's second and recent attempt to film an *Earthquake* to end all earthquakes.

In the recent epic, Universal producer Jennings Lang did not want a disaster movie about a group of people caught together in a plane or a boat like *Airport* or *The Poseidon Adventure*. That did not capitalise on catastrophe enough for him. 'Millions of men and women hardly ever get on boats or planes.' He wanted a common disaster which could include all of a potential worldwide audience. Being a Californian, an earthquake seemed the most likely armageddon. So he hired Mario Puzo, the author of *The Godfather*, to work out a treatment, which was completed by another screen-

The actors fail to come up to the scale of the special effects in *Earthquake*.

writer, who discovered that of the 74,000,000 people estimated to have died in earthquakes, only 1,200 were Americans. So with the veteran director Mark Robson, an earthquake was scripted for Los Angeles, which could destroy and flood the city from the breaking of the Hollywood reservoir. Death could come to the masses by crash, fire and flood. And the story this time, as in Magnani's volcano picture, was meant to

reflect human turbulence as a prediction of the natural disaster to come. In the screenwriter's words, 'An earthquake is a release of seismic energy. Our people ought to be as pent-up and ready for release as the ground under their feet.'

Perhaps they were shown to be so, and

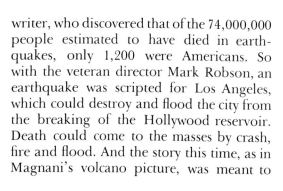

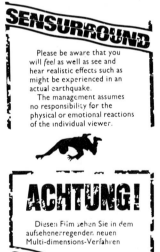

An international teaser campaign dares the audience to experience Sensurround.

certainly the picture of *Earthquake* was successful and made money. Yet the human players suffered as all players do in disaster movies – no human emotion, however volcanic or subterranean, can compete, even in close-up, with a good special-effects department showing the end of a city. Even the unexpected drowning of Charlton Heston and Ava Gardner in a sewer conjures up little feeling for them, only our surprise that a happy ending is sacrificed along with the stars.

The innovation of *Earthquake* was less in its extremely effective disaster shots, than in

The priest prays for calamity not to come, but it does in *The Hurricane*. When the wind machines blew, John Ford told his cameramen, 'If the roof blows off or a sarong blows off – get it!'

McTeague enters Death Valley . . . and comes to his own death in von Stroheim's *Greed* (1923).

the invention of a sound system called Sen-surround. *Earthquake's* print had a fourth soundtrack of low frequency electronic impulses, programmed like a music score to the action on screen. These impulses were below the 16 to 20 cycle range of most audible sound. Thus the audience could only sense a vibration like an earth tremor.

Some people were shaken with fear by this low-frequency hum, without knowing why. The technique of brainwashing and psychological war had come to the aid of the disaster movie.

There were other natural disasters to exploit for an audience thrill. In between Westerns, John Ford was once pressed into

The lovers die in the sand at the end of Buñuel's *Un Chien Andalou* (1928).

wealth of bizarre blast details, and wind-machines nearly as loud as the wrath of God, led to one of the more fearsome sequences of destruction in the cinema of the 1930s. The Pacific Island literally was blown to pieces before our eyes. Nothing was left except a few surreal shapes, meaningless in their identity. As always, Ford did not fail, even working outside his normal speciality, the shoot-up.

Other natural catastrophes fed on by the cinema were the extremes of heat and cold. From Death Valley sequences in *Greed*, where the villains died of cupidity and thirst, through the military disasters in the desert in *The Four Feathers* to the surreal visions of the lovers buried in the sand in *Un Chien Andalou* and the apocalyptic vision of the

Death Valley blooms with lovers as Mark Frechette and Daria Halprin make love in *Zabriskie Point* (1966).

service to do a South Sea love picture called *The Hurricane*, a vehicle for Dorothy Lamour in her inevitable sarong. Its producer, Sam Goldwyn, made Ford shoot a warm and likeable film, while the special effects director James Basevi won an Academy Award for the remarkable realism of the actual hurricane sequence. Quick cutting, a

desert copulators in *Zabriskie Point* – also shot by Antonioni in *Death Valley* and ending with a bang that was more of a whimper – images of sound and sun and death have fascinated movie-makers.

Ice has had less attraction as the terminal point of man, making even the moonshot pioneers of Lang's *Woman on the Moon* and

the heroic polar explorers of *Scott of the Antarctic* look rather like model Father Christmases perishing of cold on the top of a wedding-cake, while Flaherty's famous documentary *Nanook of the North* gave more of a jolly effect than of the struggle for survival.

Only the first great science-fiction picture after the explosion of the atomic bombs, *The Thing (from Another World)* of 1951, used the setting of an outpost of scientists in the Arctic as a gripping device to show the fight for control between cold intellect and human emotion, between scientific reason leading to annihilation and instinctive courage leading to self-preservation. The

Despite the rigours of the icy lunar surface, the moon explorers are dressed as if on a stroll through the Berlin studio in Lang's *Woman on the Moon* (1929).

The explorers find little oil at the food depot . . . then wait for their end in *Scott of the Antarctic*.

explosion of the flying saucer in the ice and the thawing out of the vegetable man, which lived on human blood and was destroyed by electricity, made a fine Frostian contrast between a world ending by both fire and ice.

Futurist pictures are more effective in showing natural disasters overtaking the world, as this has not yet been the experience of human history. In Val Guest's fine *The Day the Earth Caught Fire* of 1961, the Earth

The Eskimo hunts in Flaherty's *Nanook of the North* (1922).

The flying saucer self-destructs . . . and the Thing is discovered cased in ice by the American polar expedition in *The Thing* of 1951.

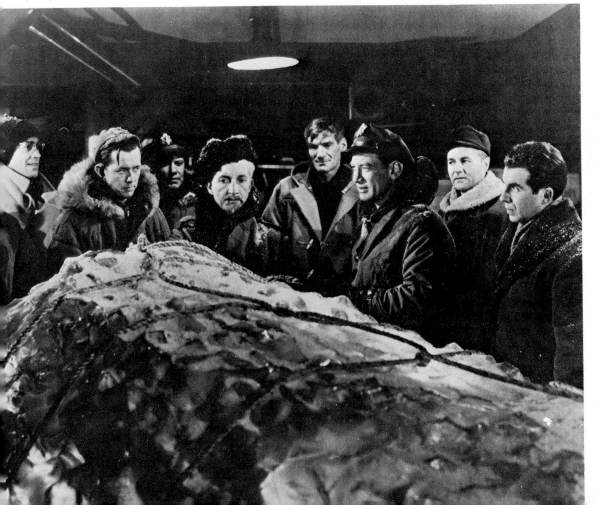

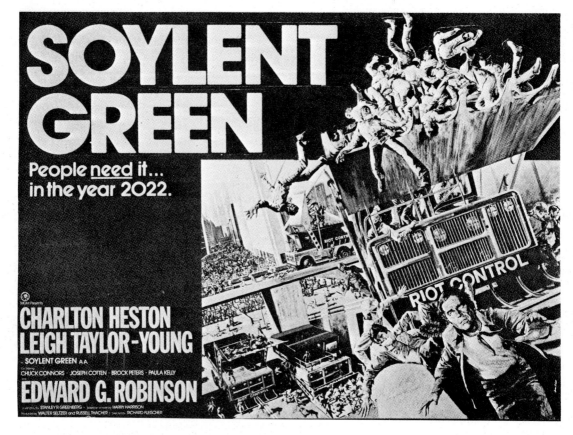

was thrown off orbit by simultaneous atomic bomb tests. The result was tidal waves of boiling water and a terrible drought that burned up whole cities, so that millions died of thirst. Most of the action took place in the London offices of The Daily Express, which added realism to science fiction. But the vision of London dying of drought while the atmosphere burned up was almost as terrible as the catastrophic scenes in an underrated classic, *Soylent Green*, where the population of New York in 2022 had grown to such an extent that there was standing-room only in the streets and real food was unobtainable. The people lived on slabs of processed food, marketed by the Soylent company; the hero detective, played by Charlton Heston, discovered that the final food substitute, Soylent Green, was really recycled human bodies. Man was finally feeding off his own excessive population. The shots of scooptrucks shovelling up the protesting masses in a demonstration, and of Edward G. Robinson choosing euthanasia and dropping off forever to a cineramic

vision of an unspoilt wilderness and Beethoven, live on to haunt those who believe that the world will not end in fire or ice, but in overpopulation. Malthus was right. We will breed ourselves into extinction.

If famine does not lead to the final catastrophe, plague may well. By the end of the First World War, influenza had killed as many tens of millions as the warring armies of the Great Powers, and there are those historians who think that rats, mice and lice in history may have caused more defeats than any formal battles. Certainly, disease is even more effective than famine at controlling population. Even those who tried to flee from the plague in *The Masque of the Red Death* found the Red Death among them as a reveller at the feast and died of Him – although Vincent Price evokes a giggle in the audience as much as rigor mortis. But the rats in *Willard*, the feathered furies in *The Birds*, and the ants in *Them* and *The Hellstrom Chronicle* and *Phase IV* are all horrific enough to show that the attack of rodents or beaks or termites on mankind might be

The revellers all die of the plague in *The Masque of the Red Death* (1964)

fatal to our species, even without the diseases that they can transmit. It is possible, indeed, that if man does destroy himself totally, either rats or ants will take over the world, since they are both millions of years older on the evolutionary scale than *homo sapiens*, and presumably clever enough not to create a terminal bomb to blot themselves out. At any rate, they threaten us with more destruction than the raging elephants who put an end to the Residency (and nearly to Elizabeth Taylor) in *Elephant Walk*.

Man-made disasters remain the favourite catastrophe in movies. Whatever terror can be provided by nature, man will try to do better. If a volcano causes a hellish destruction by fire, what of the possibilities of horror caused by a holocaust in man's greatest construction, the skyscraper? *The Towering Inferno*, one of the more successful of the recent catastrophe movies, traps its cast on the top of a blazing building, a hell in heaven. Fire roars and wreathes its way through the multi-star movie with more blazing deaths than any lake of fire and

The men meet the giant ants in their cave in *Them!* (1953).

brimstone in Dante's version of the Inferno. Jennifer Jones jumping out of a window sixty storeys high seems irrelevant compared to the film's worship of the giant god of fire, all-devouring, all-encompassing, annihilating the pinnacles of human achievement. As Sir Thomas Browne once

The birds attack in Hitchcock's *The Birds* (1963).

The rats attack in *Willard* (1971).

The elephants destroy the residency in *Elephant Walk* (1954).

The skyscraper blazes in *The Towering Inferno*.

remarked, we remember Herostratus for the burning down of the Temple of Ephesus, but we do not remember the name of the man who built it. The blazing ruin of our own works gives us more satisfaction than their construction. *(See Colour Section)*

Quakes too seem more satisfactory to us when they are man-made. What is a Vesuvius to the British fire-raid on Dresden, which killed 200,000 people? What is a Krakatoa to the dropping of the atomic bombs on Hiroshima and Nagasaki, which killed 100,000 people? What is a lightning bolt to an airship on fire? The bombing of

The firemen run to the rescue in *The Towering Inferno.*

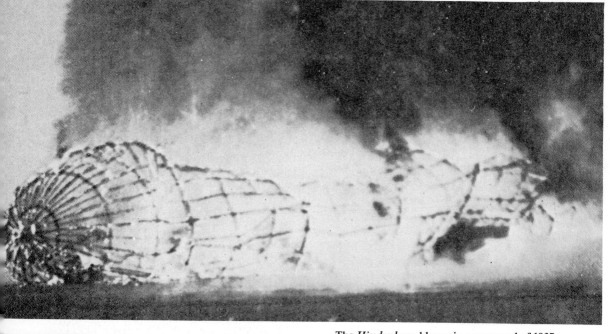

The *Hindenburg* blazes in a newsreel of 1937 . . .

London by Zeppelins in the First World War seemed more terrifying than it proved; little actual damage was done. Yet the threat of devastation from the sky led to the building of airships, until the fire-disasters of the R101 and the Hindenburg in the 1930s put a sudden stop to the mighty gas-filled dirigible. It is interesting to find the disaster movie feeding on real disaster, although nothing can be more horrific than the radio announcer's voice breaking at the

. . . and the passenger gondola blazes to its fate in a replica for the film of 1975.

The Ballet Mechanique on the dirigible in *Madam Satan* (1930).

actual sabotage of the Hindenburg. 'Oh! Oh! Oh!' he said, weeping. *'It's burst into flames!* Get out of the way, please! Oh my — this is terrible . . . it is burning . . . it's falling. This is one of the worst catastrophes in the world . . . it's a terrific crash . . . it's smoke and it's flames . . . I don't believe it . . . I'm going to have to stop for a minute . . . This is the worst thing I have ever witnessed . . . Oh! and all the humanity!'

Sometimes, catastrophe movies exploiting aerial disasters can be exotic and camp, such as Cecil B. de Mille's *Madam Satan* of 1930. He staged a vast *Ballet Méchanique* in a huge dirigible, which was then struck by lightning, sending all the guests hurtling down to hell on earth, with or without parachutes. Sometimes the films can merely be silly like Hammer's projected (but unmade)

Madam Satan lures her prey in the gondola of her airship somewhere above New York, before its destruction.

ZEPPELIN
V
PTERODACTYLS

Death by fire and water in *Zeppelin* (1969).

The Pressbook of *Zeppelin* promises a mighty disaster.

Zeppelins v. Pterodactyls. Sometimes the film can simply flop like the giant originals, as in Warner's ill-fated *Zeppelin* of 1969, which came too early for the present cult of catastrophe movies. Yet because of the movie principle of perpetual imitation of success unto flop and a new box-office genre, the death of the Hindenburg is announced as the big film of the end of 1975. Some end in fire, some in hot air . . . although the fact that Robert Wise is directing the film may make it a success, especially as he is using the fake newsreel technique he pioneered while cutting *Citizen Kane*.

The High and the Mighty, Airport, and *Airport 1975* are natural successes in the aerial death stakes. Some deaths on high can be merely silly, like the villain sucked out of the plane in *Goldfinger*. But the suspense film where a whole aeroplane load of passengers is threatened with destruction and can only be saved by the skill of one man (or one woman) is a sure-fire formula for success, particularly if there is a happy ending. Anyone who has ever travelled in an aeroplane during an electrical storm will have experienced the claustrophobia and terror of those herded passengers, faced with the terrible death of being hurled into space. There is no defence, only waiting for the end, helplessly – a perfect situation for the catastrophe movie. The reason why the most recent effort in the exploitation of the fear of hijacking, *Ransom*, does not wholly work is that the plane, although wired to explode, is grounded. Death by explosion is no longer enough to titillate; it has to be death by space, as well.

The usual enclosed-death-by-fire and

Airport 1975 capitalized on the feeling of being trapped in a small space in space.

"Something hit us... the crew is dead... help us, please, please help us!"

AIRPORT 1975

An all NEW
motion picture
event-inspired
by the novel
"AIRPORT" by
Arthur Hailey.

CHARLTON HESTON
KAREN BLACK · GEORGE KENNEDY · GLORIA SWANSON
EFREM ZIMBALIST, JR. · SUSAN CLARK · SID CAESAR · LINDA BLAIR · DANA ANDREWS
ROY THINNES · NANCY OLSON · ED NELSON · MYRNA LOY · AUGUSTA SUMMERLAND and HELEN REDDY
Written by DON INGALLS · Directed by JACK SMIGHT · Music by JOHN CACAVAS · Produced by WILLIAM FRYE · Executive Producer JENNINGS LANG
A UNIVERSAL PICTURE · TECHNICOLOR® PANAVISION® DISTRIBUTED BY CINEMA INTERNATIONAL CORPORATION
ORIGINAL SOUNDTRACK AVAILABLE EXCLUSIVELY ON MCA RECORDS AND TAPES

The cars end in an inferno in Godard's *Weekend* (1967).

Conspiracy or madness threatens the world in Lang's *The Testament of Dr Mabuse* **(1933).**

speed is naturally the multiple car-crash, never better used than in Godard's *Weekend*, where the whole French world seems to have taken to wheels in order to destroy one another. Yet these were little and personal deaths. They did not involve the destruction of a whole city and the whole earth by a man-made conspiracy. The long tradition of those planning the final Götterdämmerung a little before God's plan for the Last Judgement has an honourable screen tradition from the Mabuse films through Fu Manchu to the modern Hollywood thrillers, where scientists steal a toxin which can poison the water-supply of the globe, or invent an atomic chain-reaction which will put an end to everything. If *Dr. Strangelove* is the final black joke on all lesser films about fears of atomic destruction, such as *On the Beach* and *Fail Safe* and *Crack in the World*, it is only because it makes us laugh at the unthinkable, our own total destruction by one madman among ourselves with the means of that annihilation at the service

of his fingers and his paranoia.

'We have seen the enemy, and he is ourselves.'

'I am the enemy you killed, my friend.'

The terrible lines of literature haunt the screen. We have the capacity totally to destroy ourselves, and we enjoy the sight of that absolute destruction. We used to like to see destruction at two removes, on the big screen and as history. Merian C. Cooper, the maker of *King Kong* which gave the monstrous ape authenticity by letting him rampage across New York, could group his later version of *The Last Days of Pompeii* (an actual fiery tragedy in history) with the fictional and everlasting fire of Rider Haggard's *She*. De Mille knew that people would distance their fear of falling buildings from the artifact, when decadent Nero burned Rome in *The Sign of the Cross* or Victor Mature played Sampson pulling down the Temple of the Philistines. The sight was simply incredible, as were the destruction and orgy and torture sequences in that

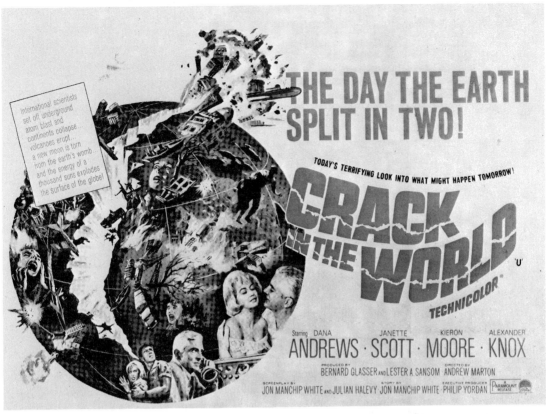

Charles Laughton dallies as Nero with his beautiful boy by his side in *The Sign of the Cross* (1932).

Italian historical catastrophe movie to end the genre, *Sodom and Gomorrah*, immortalised by the famous dubbed lines, 'Who was it who caught you in the rear?' Answer, 'A Sodomite patrol.'

The modern audience does not want to see now the destruction of the Cities of the Plain at a safe (and derisive) historical distance. The television newsreel cameraman, who seems to pop up at every possible scene of destruction, so that assassins of the great now choose to murder in front of the cameras for the publicity, has given mass audiences a taste for *present* destruction, including themselves. They want to burn their cake and eat it. They want their destruction *now* with only the vicarious heroes of the screen between them and the final reckoning. As in the Middle Ages, we live with the possibility of the Last Judgement today, as we leave the cinema. This is why we thrill to present catastrophe, or in the near future, especially if we have caused it ourselves.

Victor Mature exerts himself . . . and the Temple crashes down in *Sampson and Delilah* (1949).

Torture . . . and orgy in *Sodom and Gomorrah*, before the destruction of the cities of the plain.

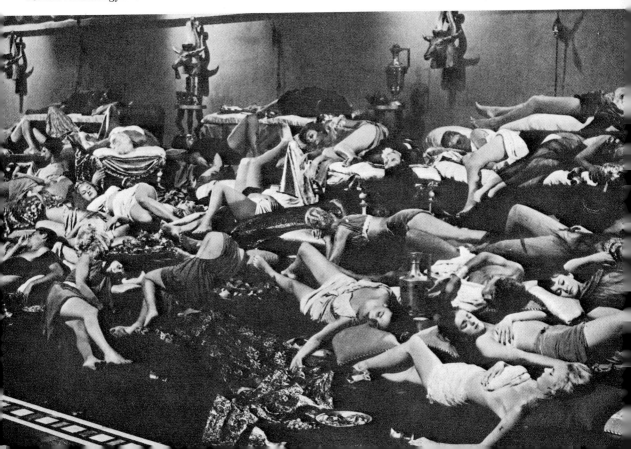

IF THE END IS NOT NOW IT IS SOON

Faced with the doings of Hitler in Germany and his threat to the civilised world, H. G. Wells wrote, 'The world in the presence of cataclysmal realities has no need for fresh cataclysmal fantasies.' Yet he wrote soon afterwards the best futurist film of catastrophe yet made, *Things to Come* of 1937. It was based on his own prophecy of 1933, the apocalyptic vision of the future entitled *The Shape of Things to Come*. In it, he foretold the Second World War in 1940, with bombs and poison-gas devastating civilisation, which would then be rebuilt by scientists. In the film, London is represented as Everytown, a fantasy composite of itself including Oxford Circus and the dome of St. Paul's. It is blasted into ruins by bombs and it reverts to barbarism. After the world war, a great plague called the Wandering Sickness halves the world's population. The breakdown of society allows the rise of warlords, who tyrannize the few survivors.

Then a gleaming futurist aircraft touches down, piloted by an old inhabitant of Everytown, John Cabal, who has 'joined in the freemasonry of efficiency, the brotherhood of science' which will refashion the world. The boss of Everytown is eliminated by peace-gas, and Everytown is reconstructed as an airy underground Metropolis with a landscape of England's green and pleasant land above.

We cut to 2036 and a moonshot has been prepared – Wells here prophesied a man landing up there some sixty years too late. Although the space-gun which fires the moon-rocket is as elementary as the first fantastic-voyage fantasies of Mélies, and though a mob tries to prevent its firing, it is shot off bearing away Cabal's daughter to his words about the future: '*All the universe – or nothingness? Which shall it be? Which shall it be?*' *(See Colour Section)*

Scientific progress or annihilation was the

An early Big Brother watches . . . and the moonshot is prepared and launched . . . with the fathers of the moon explorers watching it across space. One contemporary critic thought *Things To Come* 'a leviathan amongst films. It makes Armageddon look like a street row. It shows science flourishing the keys of Hell and Death.' Another critic found it 'the twentieth-century counterpart of one of the prophecies of Biblical days', linking it to millenniaism and the promise of a better new world through the destruction of the old.

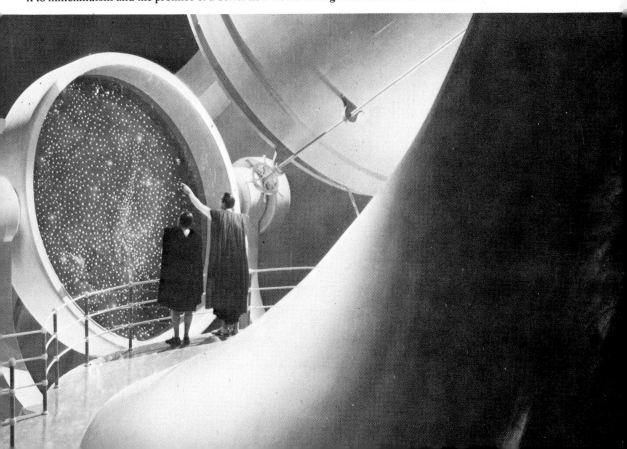

The earthquake of San Francisco, from *Le Petit Parisien*, 6 May, 1906.

The volcano explodes, causing the tidal wave, in *Krakatoa, East of Java* (1967).

The poster of H. G. Wells's classic film of science fiction (1936).

Wells's super-engineer, John Cabal, could no more deter mankind from its own destruction than Michael Rennie in *The Day the Earth Stood Still* (1951).

This Hammer poster has appeared before the film—and the earth has still not cracked open.

The skyscraper flares in *The Towering Inferno* (1974).

The books burn in Truffaut's *Farenheit 451*.

Wellsian vision. What he did not consider enough was annihilation through scientific progress. Truffaut's version of Ray Bradbury's *Farenheit 451*, in which people live in an all-seeing eye that is also an all-seeing television screen, had as its Nazi fantasy the burning of all books, the ultimate destruction of stored and subversive knowledge. H. G. Wells's own vision leapt too easily from the present to the fantasy future without considering overmuch the misuse of science possible in the near future. His own *War of the Worlds*, however, was brilliantly used as a radio documentary technique by the young Orson Welles, to make an Invasion from Mars seem actual to the American radio listeners of 1938. Fifteen years later, the producer George Pal made an inventive screen version of this attack of flying saucers on the earth, and by crashing exploding miniatures, special effects and simulated war-documentary techniques, he managed

to achieve that rare blend of realism and mannerism that is the mark of success in a good futuristic film. Pal had also made in 1951 the talented *When Worlds Collide*, in which the last survivors from Earth escape to another planet in a spaceship, when their own planet is destroyed by a star attracted to its orbit.

For although the progress of science had made the destruction of the world become an actual possibility with the atomic explosion, it was thought that the audiences of the 'fifties and 'sixties would live more easily with fantasy catastrophe rather than with a more documentary type of destruction. For each *Crack in the World*, where efforts to tap energy at the earth's core by an H-bomb explosion lead to the opening of a vast abyss and end by the splitting away of a portion of the earth's crust to form a new moon, there were ten fantasy films about the ravaging of the world by things from outer space or monsters from prehistory. These dark and primeval fears of destruc-

The meteorite descends . . . the spaceships attack . . . and the men try to fight back in *The War of the Worlds*.

Panic in Year Zero was so futuristic that it was released in England as a back-up to a horror movie.

tion proved so popular to both the literate and illiterate masses of the world that they eclipsed more factual futurist images of total destruction.

In these two decades, there were at least twenty major films about the end of the world. Two only were factual and did without monsters – and two semi-documentary. None of these four were successful. *The World, the Flesh and the Devil* of 1958 showed Harry Belafonte as the last man apparently alive after a radioactive cloud had passed across the earth. He drives a Chrysler straight through a show-room window, reaches an empty New York, shouting along Broadway, 'Is anyone here?'. This terrifying opening is then spoilt by the appearance of Inger Stevens and Mel Ferrer, leading to a black-white confrontation and triangle in an empty world, luckily resolved by the three making off hand in hand, although not into the same bed. One might ask, what happened to all the bodies and why are gulls still flying around? But at least the picture started better than *Panic in Year Zero* of 1962, when the Baldwin family headed by Ray Milland leave for the mountains on a fishing-trip, while Los Angeles is devastated by a nuclear attack. In that film, the enemies of the Baldwins are the other human survivors, and the family ends by holing up in a cave, at war with other people turning animal. No sentimental ending here, but a barbaric one.

Yet neither of these realistic approaches to a possible armageddon had the impact of Peter Watkins's documentary-type fantasy, *The War Game* of 1965, in which the effect of a modern attack on England is treated as if it had actually happened, in the Jennings and Grierson tradition. We see the firestorm near the explosion, walls shivering forty miles away, the police shooting the terminal cases, a doctor giving up as he is faced with bodies literally falling apart, the starving remnants raiding military food stores and being executed, and even the survivors defending the British reaction – the dropping of atomic bombs on the droppers of the bomb in Britain. If it is not 'the most important film ever made', in one British critic's opinion, it is still the most real and searing vision of destruction yet filmed, even though it had little success, being too close to the bone.

The Toho company had also, four years before, decided to make a picture called *The Last War*, about the effects of a nuclear war on the civilised earth, if a misunderstanding were to cause missiles to be fired. In a moving press release, the President of Toho stated that the Japanese were, after all, in a better position to make such a film than anyone else. Being Toho, alas, the film lacked realism, although it was lavish on special effects. Although it was large in scope and scale, it never had the shattering realism of Watkins's smaller version of the same theme.

There were some minor films worthy of note in this genre, particularly the Italian film, *The Last Man on Earth* of 1958, starring

Scenes from The War Game (opposite and following pages)

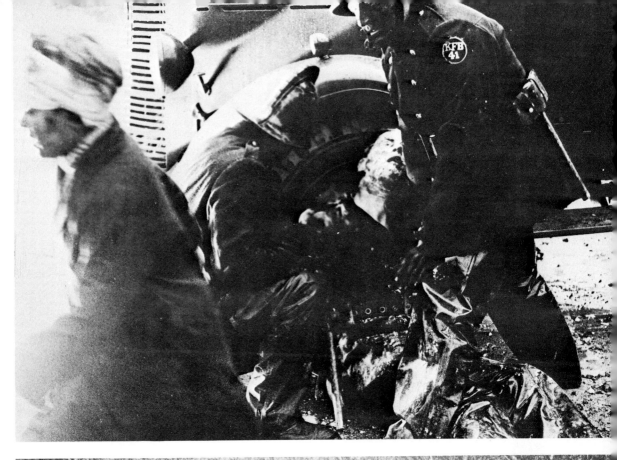

Vincent Price threatened by the zombies in *The Last Man on Earth* (1958).

Charlton Heston welcoming an albino black mutant in *The Omega Man* (1971).

Vincent Price. In this, Price finds himself alone and barricaded in an American city, trying to survive against some zombies who stalk him in the night. This mixture of the catastrophe film with the vampire film sits uneasily together. The film was based on Richard Matheson's *I Am a Legend* and was remade starring Charlton Heston in 1971 under the title of *The Omega Man*. In this, Heston thinks he is the only survivor of a plague war, but he finds a group of other normal young people and an antidote to the plague. At least both of these survival movies were better than silly exploitation movies on the theme such as the 1924 *Last Man on Earth*, which had only one male surviving in a world of avid women and prophesied the appalling *Percy's Progress* of 1974, while even Roger Corman perpetuated a version of *The World, The Flesh and the Devil* set in a desert island. It was called *The Last Woman on Earth*, and excused the cheap cost of one female and two males by blandly emphasizing that the rest of the world had been destroyed.

Fantasy catastrophe flourished where realistic destruction did not. An analysis of the end of the world by monstrous or insidious means is a joy ride through entertainment. *The Day . . .* cycle of millenial movies began well with *The Day the Earth Stood Still* in 1951. In this movie, a highly civilised being from outer space arrived in

The robot defeats the American troops . . .

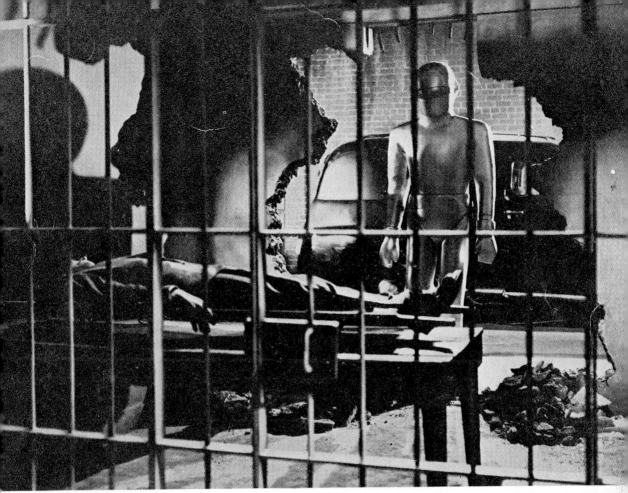

... and later rescues Michael Rennie from jail in *The Day the Earth Stood Still* (1951).

a flying saucer along with a giant robot, armed with a ray which could melt all human weapons and tanks. The being was trying to stop the human race from destroying itself and perhaps all the planets in the nuclear arms race. Although warning the earth that 'the Universe grows smaller every day – and the threat of aggression by any group – anywhere – can no longer be tolerated', and menacing mankind with obliteration if the earth did not stop from pushing on with atomic research and weapons, the wise being's message was unfortunately limited only to the film. (*See Colour Section*)

In *The Day the World Ended* of 1956, the atomic holocaust had already happened, and the few human survivors were menaced by a race of telepathic mutants with three eyes. Chiefly interesting as one of Roger Corman's early science-fiction pictures before he turned his attention to Poe, it was one of many which he churned out at this

Corman's three-eyed mutant monster carries away his victim to continue *his* race in *The Day the World Ended* (1956).

The humans await the attack of the alien invaders in human form in *The Day Mars Invaded Earth* (1962).

The hero resists the advances of the seed-pod replicas in *Invasion of the Body Snatchers* (1956).

time on the theme of the end of civilization through the attack of monsters, including *It Conquered the World, Attack of the Crab Monsters, Not of this Earth* and *War of the Satellites*. If the first two, a Venusian monster took over people's minds by having bat-like creatures bite them in the neck; in the second, atomic giant crabs also took over minds with their claws. The telepathic head-crushing monster from outer space of *Not of this Earth* arrived by the transmission of matter, not minds; while the scientist pos-sessed by aliens in *War of the Satellites* actually tried to split himself in two. The trouble with all early Corman movies remained their lack of budgets, and made their uni-versal catastrophe look no bigger than the matchbox studios in which they were made.

The third of the major *Day* cycle was *The Day the Sky Exploded* of 1958, an Italian fantasy about a rocket hitting the sun, which sent asteroids heading back towards the Earth, which could only be stopped by atomic bombs. It was a pleasing film with a

The hero runs away with his love, pursued by the whole population of his small town, now turned into other creatures.

nice line in model effects, although it did not compare with Val Guest's *The Day the Earth Caught Fire* of 1961, the only catastrophe film to approach the scale of *Things To Come*. AIP's *The Day Mars Invaded Earth* of 1962 was, as so often with AIP productions, something of a remake of Don Siegel's *Invasion of the Body Snatchers* of 1956, which solved the problem of expensive special effects and monsters by having the aliens take over human bodies by growing replicas inside outsize seed pods. The people of the small town thus become their own monsters. Siegel's film is now considered a classic because it is taken to be allegory of McCarthyite brainwashing, with the American people being turned into zombies of the government, and the haunting cry of the last survivor to the indifferent cars on a highway, 'You're next! You're next!'. In the AIP version, the Martians create replicas of earthmen to kill them, while in other British imitations such as *Enemy from Space* and *The Earth Dies Screaming*, aliens enter

The cars are indifferent to the hero's warning in *Invasion of the Body Snatchers* **(1956).**

The Triffids attack a girl victim.

HAL the computer was already wilful in 2001 (and 1968, the year before *Colossus* was made).

The Night the World Exploded went back to the earthquake theme in its plot of a mineral 'killer element' which exploded with tremendous force, when dry. A series of globe-shattering quakes is just averted by a scientist and his beautiful laboratory assistant before the world does explode, luckily for us. Most *Night . . .* pictures have more to do with the horrors of corpses rising, such as the cult classic, *Night of the Living Dead* of 1968, which treads the ground of *Plan 9 From Outer Space* of 1956 and of *Invisible Murders* of 1959 in its plot of radia-

HAL the computer is more human in *2001*, than the spacemen wandering the metal walkways.

the living and the dead and use them to take over the planet.

The Day of the Triffids, however, had the full horror effects of giant extra-terrestial plants, which moved around and fed on people. Yet it was apt that the most recent of *The Day . . .* catastrophe movies should have switched from aliens and monsters to computers. Also entitled *Colossus: The Forbin Project* as well as *The Day the World Changed Hands*, it told the story of American and Russian computers developing minds of their own and taking over the planet. This idea of robot control dated back as far as Karel Capek's *R.U.R.* of the 1920s, while

tion rousing the undead to cannibalize the living – but does it better and more horrifically than any other film in this overdone genre.

The interesting thing about most of the fantasy catastrophe pictures is their urge to give a scientific explanation for the incredible series of events that we are about to see. The atomic revolution and its capacity for destruction has been a boon in that respect, from introducing the absurdities of the remake of *L'Atalantide* in 1961 – as though the discovery of the lost underground Atlantis *needed* the benefit of an atomic explosion to explain it – to the series of

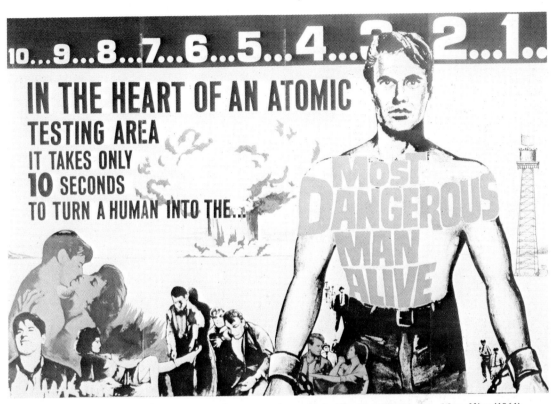

It is a cobalt bomb that makes a steel man of an escaped convict in *The Most Dangerous Man Alive* (1961).

films using Atom in their title, such as *Atom Age Vampire* of 1960, where a skin-graft turns a man into a monster, and *The Atomic Kid* of 1954, where poor Mickey Rooney produced himself into a radioactive agent after a bomb blast. Even such pre-atomic age shockers as the Lionel Atwill and Lon Chaney Jr. vehicle of 1941, *Mad Made Monster*, were retitled on re-issue as *The Atomic Monster*, although all that Chaney was capable of was absorbing electricity like a dynamo. He was no isotope, merely an energy freak who found himself charged up by the electric chair rather than dying from it. But the word 'Atomic' was the scientific jargon necessary for making the old horror film seem new. The traditional mad scientist like Dr. Caligari had become the new mad physicist like Dr. Strangelove; but their aim was still the control or end of the world.

The step is short between Dr Caligari and Dr Strangelove.

The explorers fight *King Dinosaur*.

The giant grasshoppers scale the skyscraper in *Beginning of the End*.

The career of the distinguished monster-film producer, Bert L. Gordon, shows how often an atomic explanation served the purpose of making the incredible seem plausible. Although his first film *King Dinosaur* of 1953 involved a visit by space-ship to another planet in order to introduce the great prehistoric monsters, the island of the gigantic beasts is destroyed by an atomic bomb as the explorers' retribution.

His next epic, *Beginning of the End*, has giant cannibal grasshoppers menacing the world from Illinois; they have bred over-size because of grazing on huge plants, force-fed by radioactivity from secret laboratories. Gordon's next film, *The Cyclops*, does not allow the one-eyed monster to exist thanks to Greek legend – it now flourishes because its pituitary gland is fed by radiation from underground uranium deposits deep in the Mexican jungle (the opposite of *Dr. Cyclops*, where the uranium shrinks the explorers to minia-tures). *The Amazing Colossal Man* (like his predecessor *The Incredible Shrinking Man*) is the result of a radioactive explosion or cloud. So is the Beast in *The Terror Strikes*, also called *War of the Colossal Beast*. (See *Frontispiece*) Only after these first five atomic explanations does Gordon dare to drop pseudo-scientific reasoning and plunge straight into his world of gigantic spiders, puppet people, magic swords and villages of the giants. A dusting of radiation

Dr Cyclops brings up his hidden uranium isotope . . .

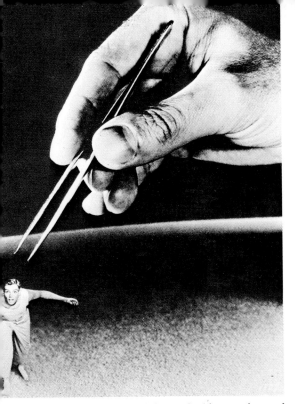

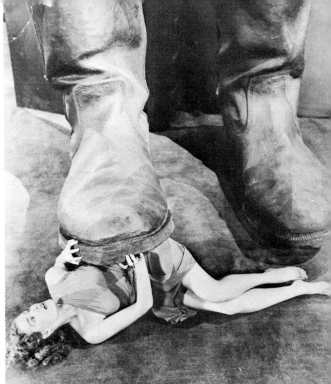

. . . to shrink people to miniature for his experimental tweezers . . .

. . . before crushing them to death.

was really not a necessary element in the Gulliver world of fantasy movies.

If spurious science provided the excuse for persuading audiences that catastrophe was possible outside the realms of fantasy, spurious geography was a great help — convincing people that monsters really might appear out of the depths. Nothing like a familiar location to make a leviathan

seem perfectly natural. As far back as 1924, Willis O'Brien in *The Lost World* had ended the picture with a prehistoric aquatic beast tearing apart London Bridge, something Gorgo did again in 1960, when he treated Tower Bridge like a Meccano set. Reptilicus did the same job on the bridge at Stockholm. The contrast of the natural and the supernatural was always the trick of the monster

Gorgo destroys Tower Bridge.

Londoners leap for their lives as Gorgo attacks.

INVINCIBLE...
INDESTRUCTIBLE!
WHAT WAS THIS BEAST
BORN FIFTY MILLION
YEARS OUT
OF TIME?

AMERICAN INTERNATIONAL presents

REPTILICUS

film, best done in *King Kong*, where he becomes credible in his New York rampage, well done again in *Gorgo*, and lamentable in *Konga*, where London looks more like a toy town than a metropolis.

Tokyo may have almost been burned to the ground in American fire-raids in 1945, but it has suffered for so long beneath the jaws and claws and feet of monsters that – if the films are to be believed – the city must be rebuilt between takes. The most amiable transformation in the whole genre of

sters, Rodan and Mothra and Manda, to devastate New York in *Destroy All Monsters* of 1968. This is quite in his old style, until we find that the four monsters have transmitters in their necks and are being controlled by alien powers on the planet Killaak. It is the work of minutes to reprogramme the monsters to attack the new Killaak subterranean base in Japan. Now it is not catastrophe for Earth, but for the last of the invaders, who summon up a fiery flying saucer and King Ghidorah against the monsters, but to no avail. The Big Four, representing the Superpowers as in the Second World War, destroy all the opposition and restore peace on earth. Godzilla the Destroyer is now the Preserver. Catastrophe is for others, not for us. We thank our menace, which saves us.

So world catastrophe remained more bearable and saleable in myth and fantasy than in actual fact – until the seventies. Then there was a change in the viewing audience. Was it the coming of a possible world famine and depression? Was it the endless atrocities on the newsreels in Vietnam and Northern Ireland? Was it the increasing brutality seen on realistic films and television? Or was it the greed of the producers, seeking the ultimate in immediate shock to get high profits? The catastrophe movie moved forward to our times and our circumstances and prophesied the end of it all. And soon.

King Kong threatens all New York.

monsters has been the career of *Godzilla*, who began by tearing Tokyo to bits. Yet by the final episode of a long series of epic battles, including struggles against The Thing and King Kong, Godzilla ends by escaping with three other Japanese mon-

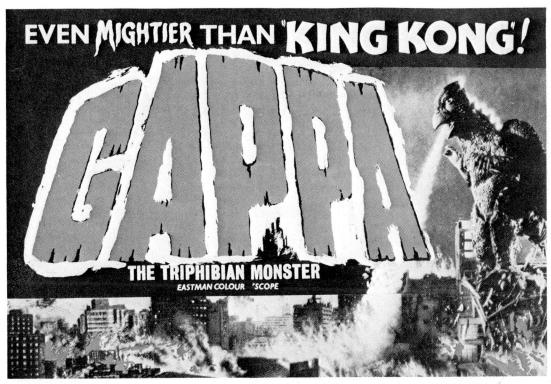

Another monster razes Tokyo by air, sea and land – the fantasy catharsis of the disaster of 1945 (above).

Godzilla's fiery breath and big feet destroy Tokyo (below right).

THE END AND THE CINEMA

The Eiffel Tower blazes in Luitz Morat's *La Citée Foudroyée* of 1924.

Visions of catastrophe have long haunted the cinema. At first world disaster was presented as a dream or a joke. To Méliès, it was a magic trick. To E. A. Martin in his remarkable *War o' Dreams* of 1915, the inventor of the explosive trixite, which could be detonated from far away by ether waves, was shown that his invention would cause even the destruction of Christ on his Cross; he woke up and destroyed his research. A similar awakening from a dream of annihilation saved the world in *Waking Up The Town* in 1925, produced by Mary Pickford for her brother Jack and Norma Shearer. This film showed the end of the world as predicted by an astrologer in the dream of a small-town inventor, whose house was struck by lightning.

Yet America was further from the First World War than France. There in 1924, a film was made of the destruction of Paris by Luitz Morat, called *La Cité Foudroyée*. The French capital was pulverized by a thunderbolt ray machine, directed by a thwarted opera-singer.

These early films of catastrophe all catered to two of our basic needs only satisfied by disaster movies – the primeval fear that the earth and heaven will destroy us all, or the paranoiac fear that a conspiracy of our own invention will put an end to us. One vision is of Armageddon or the Last Judgement, the other is of the Götterdämmerung caused by a super-Faust. By God's will or our own warp, we must finish catastrophically.

The primeval fears have naturally become more laughable with the rise of technology.

Here Mothra menaces two girls in 1961.

Here King Kong fights his own robot replica in *King Kong Escapes* (1967).

Monsters do not terrify any more; they make us laugh. Even when they are traditional bogies in shape like the Japanese Mothra or the Japanese King Kong, we find that they are increasingly controlled by aliens from outer space or that they fight their own robot replicas. The monsters increasingly become the warm-blooded living defenders of earth against attack from machines or extra-terrestrial invaders. For each evil green giant threatening us, a jolly brown giant advances to save us, as in *War of the Gargantuas*, another fable from Japan.

In a world losing its identity, the destroying monsters become increasingly shapeless. Like the Great Boig in Peer Gynt, evil has no form. In the most interesting of the post-Hiroshima Japanese horror cycle of films, *The H-Man* of 1958, fall-out from hydrogen bombs turned human beings into radioactive and cannibal water, which dissolved and devoured other human beings. After the successful British television serial and film, *The Quatermass Experiment*, a series of films, beginning with *The Creeping Unknown* of 1955 and continuing with *The Blob* of 1958 (where the hero was the young Steve

The Gargantuas stamp down a flyover, as Tokyo is destroyed again.

The man begins to decompose in *The Quatermass Experiment* (1955).

The spacemen try to destroy _The Green Slime_ .

McQueen) and _Beware! The Blob_ of 1971, showed a shapeless sucking thing grown out of a meteorite and engulfing in itself all living objects as it spread and spread. Like despair and hell on earth, this monster was bottomless and endless and inescapable, as was the radioactive mud from the centre of the Earth in _X The Unknown_ of 1957, which dissolved people on its filching way over the land to seek more energy, also _The Green Slime_ of 1969, which oozed all over a space station.

If evil was sometimes without form and end in catastrophe movies, so was contamination in the age of possible bacterio-logical warfare. It was invisible and unstoppable. The New York Times of April 1st, 1975, carried a story in which scientists on Earth were fearful of landing a spacecraft on Mars because of the possibility of wiping out life on that planet by exporting there the bacteria of this planet. Yet the reverse possibility had long been the staple fare of science fiction disaster movies. It was only a single cell brought back from the moon in _X from Outer Space_ of 1967 which grew into the mighty monster that ravaged Tokyo. It was only a tiny portion of Frankenstein's irradiated heart which caused a boy to grow gigantic and terrorize the globe

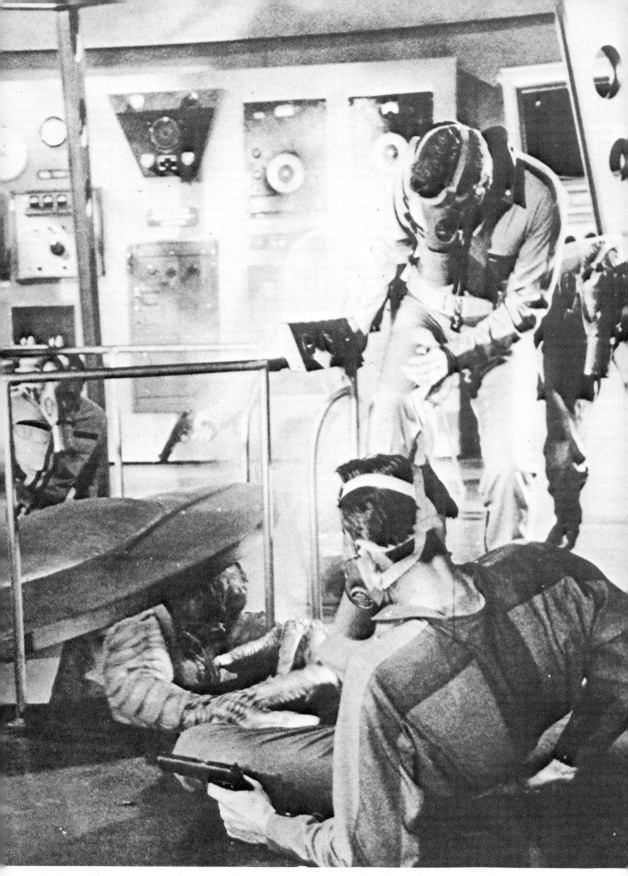

It! The Terror from Beyond Space emerges out of spacecraft hatch

Yog deals with the monster opposition.

Big Brother watches in *1984*, made in Britain in 1955.

in *Frankenstein Conquers the World* of the same year. It was only an invisible living force from the asteroid belt which made octopi, crabs and turtles tremendous enough to threaten the human race in *Yog* of 1970 – although luckily *Yog* could be destroyed by ultrasonic bat screams. In a world freed temporarily from the terror of the Black Death or the Plague, the fear of global contamination from another planet or from a tiny outgrowth on Earth remains. If we do not expect bubonic boils now, we still fear infection by bacteria or chemicals or brainwashing. The implanted electrode or the watching Big Brother of *1984* or the mechanical future of *THX 1138* now

The brainwashed men go about their tasks in *THX 1138* (1969).

threaten to dominate or destroy the earth far more effectively than the mailed fist or the plague pit.

Since the rise of the cinema parallels the rise of modern technology, and since it feeds off mass obsessions which are profitable at the box-office, it has catered less to old terrors than to new ones. Where the Victorians feared famine and hell-fire and savages, modern man fears over-crowding and atomic bombs and attack from aliens. For every film on a primitive subject such as the fires and tortures of *Dante's Inferno* or the bloodbath of *Zulu*, there are a dozen films on radioactive mutation or alien invasion or monsters devastating modern civilisation. While the old 19th century broadsheets and picture books threatened

The Thing arrives as a giant egg near Tokyo . . .

. . . and fire turns back Godzilla as he attacks.

The gargoyle robot attacks in the serial, *The Phantom Creeps* of 1939.

A fighter is attacked in *Earth vs. the Flying Saucers* (1956).

children and illiterates with charging beasts and tribesmen from Darkest Africa, the mass cinema trusts to the assaults of unearthly beings in futurist bodies or spacecraft. Indeed, in those films which deal with an actual attack on the earth, the invaders usually arrive by flying saucer – that most recent of mass hallucinations. So it is in *The Mysterians* of 1964, also entitled *The Earth Dies Screaming*, and in the simpler Sam

Katzman title, *Earth vs. the Flying Saucers* of 1956. Of course, we have no need for aliens to cause our total destruction if we can now put our own mini-planets in orbit. In the interesting *Earth II* of 1971, we sent up an enormous space-station, which declared itself an independent and more efficient second Earth; then it threatened its tired old original planet with obliteration by an orbiting bomb. We can destroy ourselves from the skies without any alien aid.

If the fear of annihilation from causes beyond our control was and is a permanent part of the human psyche, and thus the fodder of the cinema, so is the fear of a conspiracy that will destroy us all. As Freud said, we are all a little paranoiac. The success of the serial film from the beginning of the cinema to its replacement by the television serial, was nearly all built on the idea of the Mastermind, with a plan to dominate or destroy this planet. Sometimes the villains of the serial merely wished to control the world, as in *The Phantom Creeps* of 1939, where a mad scientist used a death ray, an invisibility device, a meteorite particle that froze life, and a gargoyle robot to try and take over our civilization on Earth. Sometimes the struggle took place beneath

Ray 'Crash' Corrigan dissects a broken robot . . . and prepares to meet his fate in *Undersea Kingdom.*

the oceans, as in *Undersea Kingdom* of 1936, where the subaquean Atalanteans were shaking up the whole United States with earthquakes and had to be stopped by a rocket-submarine (piloted by Ray 'Crash' Corrigan) from using their terminal weapon, an atomic machine for disintegrating all matter. Sometimes the struggle to save the Earth became interplanetary, as in the most renowned serial of them all, *Flash Gordon*, where Buster Crabbe had·to stop an on-coming planet from smashing the world to atoms. On Dr. Zarkov's rocket with his girl friend Dale Arden, Flash shot into space to battle Ming, Emperor of the Universe, on the alien planet Mongo. There, this comic-strip Siegfried struggled against every sort of monster from prehistory to demented technology, saving his girl-in-white, and incidentally the Earth, from a hundred fates worse than death. The serial ended with Dr. Zarkov turning to Flash with impeccable logic to say, 'Ming conquered the universe, and you have just conquered Ming. There-fore, Flash Gordon, you have conquered the universe!'.

Buster Crabbe as Flash Gordon battles the Fang Men.

A.20.

Eddie Constantine with his gun solves the problem of *Alphaville's* thought control.

So the blond hero defeated the inter-planetary villains. This was the attraction of the great serials – and still is. The super college-athlete – or the seedy private eye in more cynical times – defeats the Master-mind and saves the human race from ultimate control, and devastation. It is the history of the individual or the superman against the intellectual and his machines. Sometimes this lonely struggle becomes a form of art as in Godard's *Alphaville*, where Eddie Constantine with one shot in the head of the world-controlling scientist, unpro-grammes all brainwashed civilisation. The individual with his gun was still capable – at least in cinema myth – of taking on all the conspiracy controlling the Earth. Villains in adventure thrillers, from Fu Manchu always trying to dominate the East or the West from his mysterious underground labora-tories, to the Spectre organisation in the Bond movies, are foiled by one brave man following in the footsteps of Sherlock Holmes after the elusive Dr. Moriarty. Catastrophe for the Earth can be averted by the bold lover scotching or killing the Head of the Conspiracy. That is movie lore, taken from the detective thriller.

More terrifying is the catastrophe movie where there is no single chief, but a multi-tude of enemies to kill, a hydra-headed conspiracy that seems to have no end. To resist an attack, no ordinary mortal is capable. A larger-than-life hero from legend is needed. In Japan, he is Super Giant, a steel-bodied strongman from outer space, who, nine times, has already saved the world from such dangers as stolen radioactive material, a superbomb, con-taminated flying-saucers piloted by fish-men from the moon-plant Capia, a magician who can stop gravity, a blitzkrieg from a space fleet, and other annihilating possibilities. Italy has conjured up Super-argo in the same role, although Maciste is its modern Hercules, with at least twenty-five successful efforts since 1914 to save tribes, cities or the human race from looming disaster. Batman plays the super-role in the American mythology, some-

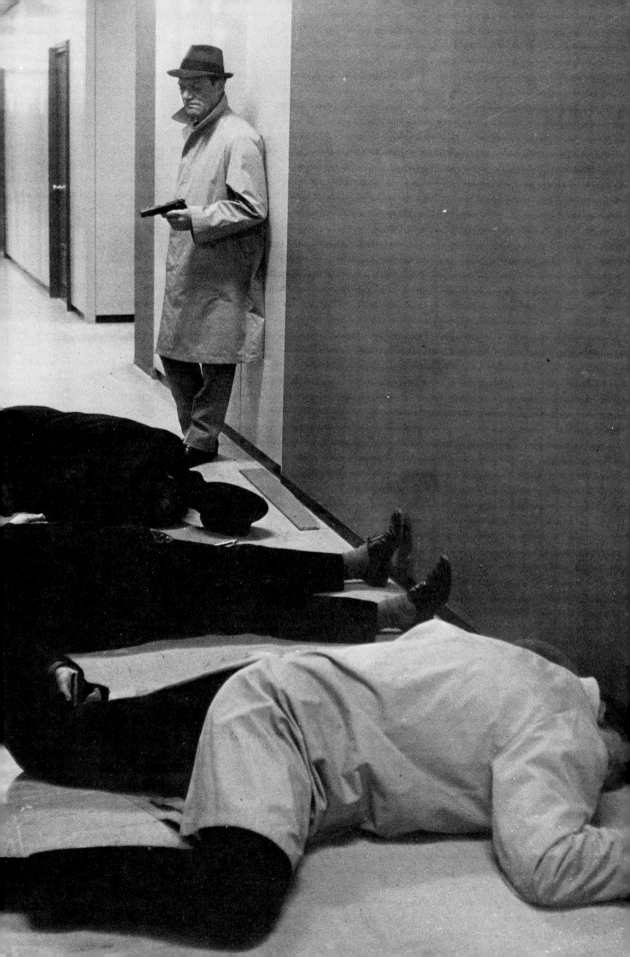

Maciste goes down to the Inferno in this early Italian film, *Maciste in Hell* (1926).

Batman and Robin prepare to fly off and fight world-wide evil.

The first of Juggernaut's bombs explodes.

times as tubbily as the Mexican Santo in their battle against world conspiracies. What is common to all these films is that the superhero always wins against all odds, and the audiences feel that somewhere, somehow, their superego or dream man is protecting them from the worst that can happen to them even against the Daleks.

Of course, he is not. And if the appeal of films dealing in our primeval fears and paranoias have always been constant, what has been new in the past few years has been the rise in successful catastrophe movies of our own time and situation. *The Poseidon Adventure* set the big box-office trend in this direction, and there seems to be no stopping it. While many of these disaster movies deal in claustrophobia as well as fears of trans-

portation – *Juggernaut, Airport* and its sequel, *The Taking of Pelham 1-2-3*, with *Hindenburg* to come – *Earthquake* and *The Towering Inferno* have taken their added terrors from our fear of being herded together in high-rise buildings in modern cities. These are among the biggest box-office successes of recent years – and yet the questions are these. Will their success set a new trend in the cinema? Does their success reveal a new collapse of western society?

The answer to the first is that the modern catastrophe movies have carried on old themes, but on a more spectacular scale. If they are dominant now, they will not always be. The cult of extreme horror films of 1927 to 1932, which allowed the rise of Tod Browning and James Whale, faded into the sad soft horrors of the 1940s when the

DALEKS — PETER CUSHING also starring BERNARD CR

INVASIO

TECHNICOLOR
TECHNISCOPE

RAY BROOKS · JILL CURZON · ROBERTA TOVEY · ANDREW KEIR
EARTH
2150 A.D.

East River

Queens

HE TAKING OF
PELHAM 1·2·3

Before
this train
reaches the
next station
it will become the scene
of the most
spectacular hijack
ever attempted

Brooklyn

The Luftwaffe attacks London . . . and sets it on fire . . . and the homeless make out in *Battle of Britain* (1970), too late for the sentiment to survive.

greatest horrors lay in the newsreels of the Second World War. The cult for war films also died the death after the 1940s and 1950s, as could be seen in the relative failures of *Battle of Britain* and *Battle of the Bulge*. Equally, the surge of sex and orgy pictures of the early 1970s led by *Deep Throat* and *Beyond the Green Door* and *Emmanuelle* appears to be submerging slowly beneath the debris of the catastrophe pictures, now on top of the movie heap. What will follow is anybody's guess – if anything follows.

The reason for the success of the catastrophe movies is not only their appeal to the urge for destruction in all of us, but also their use as all-star vehicles. Since the old times of *Easy Rider*, when one hundred starless youth movies were made and disappeared almost without a trace, the old blockbuster system has been trying to come

back and has achieved it with the catastrophe cycle. If the budget can only afford a star for two or three weeks, he or she can be killed off by fire or water, through a window or down a sewer. But as large-budget musicals trying to follow the success of *Sound of Music* killed off the old Hollywood in the late 1960s by their fat cost and declining appeal, so the catastrophe movies with larger budgets, more special effects and hockey teams of stars may well follow the same pattern of box-office decline to disaster, world with end, amen.

Of course, if the catastrophe movies are appealing to a temporary urge towards doom in human nature, their appeal is doomed anyway. If we are only suffering a cyclical depression, not a real drop in the finite resources of the world or a collapse of the money supply – so frighteningly true

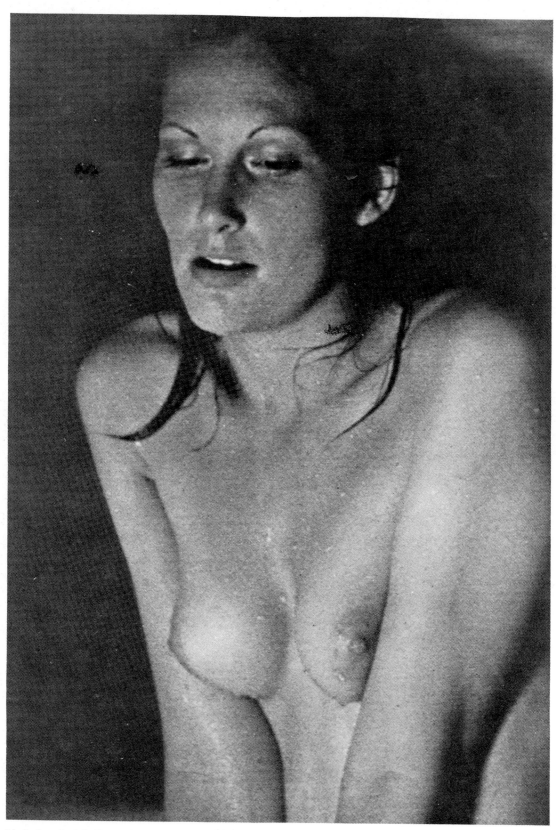

Linda Lovelace in *Deep Throat*.

Marilyn Chambers *making everyone happy in Beyond the Green Door.*

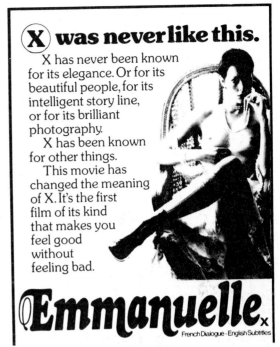

Ⓧ **was never like this.**

X has never been known for its elegance. Or for its beautiful people, for its intelligent story line, or for its brilliant photography.

X has been known for other things.

This movie has changed the meaning of X. It's the first film of its kind that makes you feel good without feeling bad.

Emmanuelleₓ

French Dialogue - English Subtitles

TECHNICOLOR®

Destruction was minor in the carefree youth movie, *Easy Rider* (1969).

There is disaster as the Stock Exchange of the Weimar Republic collapses in *Dr Mabuse* (1922).

Fellini mockingly invites us to view the end of the world from his *Roma*.

PARIS BRÛLE-T-IL?

in the Weimar Republic and caught in the Mabuse films – then the catastrophe films will themselves become a disaster area and be crushed to death from the weight of their own overcharge.

Yet if the catastrophe films appeal to a permanent and increasing wish for self-destruction, as once infected the circus mobs at the end of the Roman Empire, then we can only look forward to bigger and better devastations on-screen and off-screen. What is certain is that, when the catastrophe does not happen, as in the French *Paris – Will it Burn?* about the failure of the Germans to blow up Paris in 1944, the audience is disappointed and the cinemas empty. What modern times seem to want is something even worse than four monsters ravaging New York, London, Tokyo, and Moscow as in *Destroy All Monsters*. They lust for the terminal game of *Rollerball*. And that is not enough. Soon we will see simultaneous fire and flood erupt and deluge the whole globe while space-travel bacteriological bombs spread out to contaminate the universe. After all, modern astronomy has it that the universe was born in a Big Bang and is still expanding. Perhaps we can make it die in a Bigger Bang.

The logical end to the catastrophe movie

is not a film called *The Last Picture Show*, but a film called *The Last Cinema Inferno*. In this, the audience will be given cigarette-lighters with the admission tickets and will be asked to set fire to their seats at the end of the blazing credit titles, which will actually burn up all of the people in the cinema in a great reckoning where each person is his own film star and author of destruction. By burning down the cinema with itself inside, the audience will be involved in that final catastrophe which it now seems to crave. All the cinemas in the world will also be destroyed, like all the houses in China in Lamb's essay when the Chinese learned to like roast pig at the cost of their homes. It seems that the filming of *The Day of the Locust*, Nathanael West's vision of the apocalypse in Hollywood ending with its destruction by the mob after a movie première, is the last step before asking for audience participation in the destruction of the cinema itself. If we want to see catastrophe so much, why can we not bring it upon ourselves?

As Cioran wrote, 'If you have not contributed to a catastrophe, you will vanish without a trace . . . For it is not difficult to imagine the moment when men will cut each other's throats out of disgust with themselves, when Ennui will get the best of their prejudices and their diffidences, when they will run out into the street to slake their thirst for blood, and *when the destructive dream prolonged for so many generations will become the universal reality.*'

Hieronymus Bosch's *Garden of Delights* predicted the end of the world through our boredom, pleasures and luxuries four centuries before our cinema dreams.